The Tree Giants

The Story of the Redwoods, the World's Largest Trees

Interpreting the Great Outdoors

Illustrations by DD Dowden, text by Bill Schneider

Interpreting the Great Outdoors

Nature's wonders—such as the noble redwoods—are certainly remarkable, but unfortunately many people—especially young people—know little about them. That's one reason Falcon Press has launched this series of books called Interpreting the Great Outdoors.

Natural phenomena almost always have interesting and exciting stories behind them, stories too good to leave to scientists and naturalists. With this series of books, we hope to tell why, when, where, and how the wonders of nature came to be. We want to help satisfy the natural curiosity of our young readers.

This book is only the start. Falcon Press plans many similar books, and you can find out about them by writing us at the address below and asking to get on our mailing list for announcements of future books in the series.

Write to Falcon Press, P.O. Box 1718, Helena, MT 59624. Or call toll-free at 1-800-582-2665. You can also get extra copies of this book. Falcon Press publishes and distributes a wide variety of books and calendars so ask for our free catalog.

Copyright © 1988
by Falcon Press Publishing Co., Inc.,
Billings and Helena, Montana.

Design, illustrations, typesetting, and other prepress work by Falcon Press, Helena, Montana. Printed in Singapore.

Library of Congress Number 88-80225
ISBN 0-937959-40-5

The Tree Giants

Empires have been built and destroyed during the lifetime of a single redwood tree. Modern civilization has known of the redwood for only about 200 years. In that short time, man discovered the value of redwood for building and rapidly converted 85 percent of the majestic Coast Redwoods—almost 2 million acres of forests—into patios, decks, fences, hot tubs, siding, and other building materials. At the same time, he toppled 34 percent of the Giant Sequoias.

Fortunately, man also discovered that these remarkable trees must be protected. Through the hard work of conservationists, large forests of all three species of redwood have been set aside for enjoyment by future generations. The most remarkable trees in the world are now easily observed in many state and federal parks and in private preserves.

And so, centuries from now, the Tree Giants will still stand.

Redwoods dominated the northern hemisphere 25 million years ago, as shown here in green.

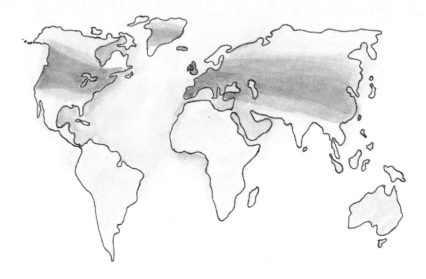

The Ancient Forests

During the Age of the Dinosaurs, redwood forests covered most of the northern hemisphere—most of what is now the continental United States, Greenland, Europe, Russia and China. The ancient forests have since fallen, but evidence of them has been preserved as fossils. Remarkably, these fossils very closely resemble today's redwoods.

Imagine the entire United States covered with redwood forests similar to those found in California's redwood parks.

But we can only imagine, as these vast forests have shrunk to less than one percent of their former size. Today, redwoods only grow along the north coast of California, on the western slopes of the Sierra Nevada Mountains, and in one remote valley in central China.

Unknown for Ages

For eons, native tribes in California lived among, used, and even worshipped the redwoods. They used redwood for canoes, for houses, and even for their clothing, which was fashioned out of the soft inner bark. Therefore, the Tree Giants were actually "discovered" long before the first Europeans cast their eyes upon the majestic trees.

The first "foreigners" to see the redwoods may have been the Chinese. Although many historians question the possibility, the captain of a Chinese junk may have been blown out to sea by a powerful storm and ended up off the California coast in 217 B.C., 1,709 years before Columbus sailed from Spain.

The Chinese trip across the Pacific also would have been at least 1,750 years before the first Spaniards traveled into Redwood Country in the early 1500s. Although the Spanish

explorers definitely saw the thick stands of Coast Redwoods, they made almost no mention of them in their journals. They were looking for gold and silver and did not get very excited about the wonders of nature. Spanish explorers also referred to the Grand Canyon as "riverbanks."

The first real mention of redwoods was made by a priest, Juan Crespi—but not until 1769 when he wandered into a thick redwood forest in the Santa Cruz Mountains. He named the tree *palo colorado*, Spanish for red wood.

It was not until 1794 that a botanist—Archibald Menzies— described the Coast Redwoods for science. And the Giant Sequoia remained hidden from science even longer. The Big Trees of the Sierra Nevada were first observed and described by Zenas Leonard, part of a 40-man exploration that crossed the Sierra Nevada in 1833.

It was the Russians who first used the redwoods for building. They settled at the mouth of the Russian River in northern California in 1812 to trap sea otters and built Ross Counter (now called Fort Ross) out of Coast Redwoods. The Russians were also the first to conduct any real logging operations on redwoods.

Even more remarkable is the late discovery of the third redwood species, the Dawn Redwood. Although local residents of a remote valley in central China knew of the Dawn Redwood for ages—just as the California Indians knew of the other two species—the rest of the world did not find out about the third redwood species until 1944.

Super Trees

Without a doubt, redwoods are super trees. They are the largest living things in the world—larger than any other tree; larger than the largest animals, including the whales; and probably larger than any plant or animal that ever lived on earth.

The Coast Redwoods have been called ''God's flagpoles'' because they soar as high as a 35-story building and grow as straight as a flagpole. They have few if any branches for the first 100 feet. The Sierra Redwood—or Giant Sequoia, as it is commonly called—is shorter and heavier. A single tree may weigh as much as 6 million pounds and contain enough wood to build 40 five-room houses.

One of the most famous trees on earth, the General Sherman Tree in Sequoia National Park, has a single branch that is larger than most trees. The branch starts 130 feet above the ground, is 21 feet around, and is 140 feet tall.

Sailors used the Coast Redwoods that grew around San Francisco Bay as landmarks—sort of like lighthouses without lights.

For many years, loggers thought redwoods were too large to cut down safely. When they finally figured out how to topple the mighty trees, the ground shook like a small earthquake each time one fell.

Despite their magnificence, the tree giants have humble beginnings. An enormous redwood can grow from a seed that weighs less than a small feather—1/8,000th of an ounce or so small that one pound contains 123,000 seeds.

Tall Tree
367.8 feet tall
14 feet in diameter

General Sherman
275 feet tall
36.5 feet in diameter

9

The Oldest of the Old

Besides being the largest living things, redwoods come close to being the oldest. Only the bristlecone pine and the Sierra juniper live longer than the majestic redwoods.

Coast Redwoods can live 2,200 years, and the Giant Sequoia can live 3,500 years or more. Some Giant Sequoias toppled by loggers in the 1800s were even said to be 4,000 years old.

That means some of the Coast Redwoods standing in California today were knee-high seedlings when Christ was born and more than 1,700 years old when George Washington was elected president. Perhaps some Giant Sequoias standing today were alive when King Tut, the boy pharoah, ruled Egypt.

But redwoods have been around much longer than that. A species

Birth of Christ

1350 B.C..
Tutankhamen

of redwood closely related to today's giants existed 125 million years ago, during the reign of the Brontosaurus and the Pterodactyl. Fossils of these trees closely resemble the redwoods of today.

How can redwood trees live so long? They have incredibly thick bark (up to one foot thick) that contains a strong chemical called tannin. This mildly acidic chemical helps the tree fight off fungi, insects, parasites and diseases. Tannin also gives the bark and wood its reddish color.

The heavy bark protects the tree from fire, and many living trees have large scars from forest fires they have survived. Unlike the bark of pine and spruce trees, redwood bark contains very little resin, which is quite flammable. The lack of resin makes redwoods more resistant to fire.

Redwoods are more durable than other trees. Buildings made of redwood have lasted more than a hundred years, such as some of those at Fort Ross, built by the Russians in northern California in 1812. Redwood coffins have been dug up a hundred years later and were almost as good as new.

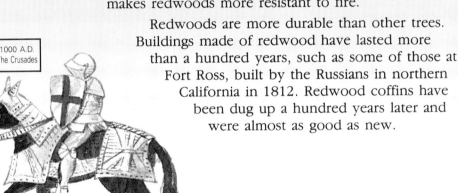

1000 A.D.
The Crusades

1969 A.D.
Man lands on
the Moon

Growth rings visible in any stump or cut log reveal a record of the tree's growth. Each ring represents a year's growth.

11

Three Redwoods

There are three species of redwoods. The Coast Redwood is tall and straight. The Giant Sequoia is slightly shorter but more massive. And the Dawn Redwood, native only to China, is smaller yet.

Loggers claim to have cut down Coast Redwoods as tall as 400 feet, but the tallest existing one soars 367.8 feet into the sky. It can be found in Redwood National Park along Redwood Creek near the town of Orick, California.

Coast Redwoods grow only along the central and northern coast of California and into the very south-western corner of Oregon. They grow straight and tall and in thick stands. Even though many thousands of these majestic trees have been cut down for timber, they are still much more numerous than the other two redwood species.

Coast Redwood

Giant Sequoia

Coast Redwood

Dawn Redwood

The Giant Sequoia does not grow as tall as the Coast Redwood, but it is bulkier. The largest Giant Sequoia is the famous General Sherman Tree in Sequoia National Park. It stretches 275 feet high and has a diameter of 36.5 feet. The General Grant Tree in nearby Kings Canyon National Park has a diameter of 40.3 feet, but it is slightly shorter at 267.5 feet.

The Giant Sequoia grows only on the western slopes of the Sierra Nevada in California. Its bark has a vivid rusty-red color, while the Coast Redwood has dark reddish-gray bark. The Giant Sequoia has less value to loggers because its brittle wood splinters into small pieces when it falls to the ground.

The Giant Sequoia is less common than the Coast Redwood, and almost all the remaining members of this species have been protected in state and federal parks.

Little is known of the third species of redwood, the Dawn Redwood. Thirty million years ago, trees very similar to the Dawn Redwood covered western North America, and now these trees can be seen as fossils in petrified forests. Scientists thought they were extinct—until the species was discovered alive in one mountain valley in central China.

One big difference between the Dawn Redwood and its American cousins is that it drops its needles every fall, after they turn from green to reddish-brown, just like an oak or elm. It is also smaller, growing to a maximum height of only 140 feet.

Giant Sequoia

Dawn Redwood

The Magic of Burls

Coast Redwoods often form burls, large knoblike lumps on the trunk or near the base of the tree. Sometimes, burls are caused when the tree is injured. But more often, they form when a bud fails to develop into a branch but continues to grow.

Burls contain many buds. If one is removed from the tree and placed in water, tiny redwood sprouts will spring from it—like sprouts from a potato. After a redwood is cut down, new sprouts often grow from the tree's burls, allowing the tree to live on.

When a burl is split into slabs, it displays a beautiful pattern. As a result, burls are often used to make tabletops, clocks and other decorations.

The Immortal Tree?

When a Giant Sequoia falls, it is dead forever. But when a Coast Redwood falls, its life does not necessarily end.

When one of these Tree Giants falls or breaks off, sprouts often emerge from the mighty stump or from burls that usually grow at the base of the tree. Even when a Coast Redwood is cut down, sprouts shoot up from the stump. Sprouts also will pop up through the thin layer of soil covering the roots and grow into mature trees.

Some of these sprouts grow into giant redwoods. Since the new tree grows from the same root system as the old, it is essentially the same tree. So, in some cases, a Coast Redwood might have been reborn many times.

In some redwood groves, four or five trees can be seen growing so close together that they seem like the same tree. In fact, they started out as sprouts from a fallen giant and grew into majestic redwoods themselves.

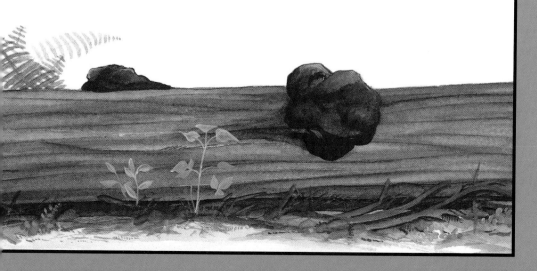

Very Fussy About
Their Living Conditions

All three redwood species need a special type of climate found in only a few places on earth. As a result, the towering giants are a rare sight.

The Coast Redwood grows only in the "coastal fog belt," a narrow strip of land about 20 miles wide stretching from the Santa Lucia Mountains just south of Carmel, California, north to the southwestern corner of Oregon.

The Coast Redwood needs a lot of moisture—from 40 to 100 inches a year. It is one of only a few plant species that actually can create its own "rain." Through a process called "transpiration," which is very much like sweating, a single tree can produce as much as 500 gallons of water a day. When an entire grove of trees transpires, it causes a steady drip of water that restores moisture to the soil.

The Coast Redwood also must have a fairly even temperature. It cannot be too hot or too cold. It prefers temperatures of 60 to 72 degrees Fahrenheit in summer and 40 to 48 degrees in winter.

The Giant Sequoia also has specific needs. The big tree needs moist, sandy soil and 45 to 60 inches of rain and snowmelt a year. Like the Coast Redwood, it does not like extreme temperatures, but it can endure weather as cold as 0 degrees Fahrenheit.

Giant Sequoias grow only in a 15-mile-wide band on the western slopes of the Sierra Nevada. They are usually found at elevations varying from 4,500 to 7,500 feet.

The Dawn Redwood grows naturally in only one valley in central China.

More Than Trees

Every forest is more than just trees, and the redwood forests are no exception. The Tree Giants are the main feature of a complex community of plants and animals, many of which depend on each other for survival.

One of the grandest animals of them all, the grizzly bear, used to rule the animal kingdom in both the Coast Redwood and Giant Sequoia forests. But now the great bear is gone. The last time one was seen in California was in 1922, near Sequoia National Park.

The grizzly's smaller cousin, the black bear, still haunts both the Sierra Nevada and the North Coast. In fact, it has become a nuisance in some parks. It has learned that campers and hikers often carry tasty food with them. The result has been ruined coolers and backpacks, torn tents, and injuries to park visitors, especially those who forget that the black bear is a wild animal.

The Giant Sequoia groves of the Sierra Nevada are probably home to more kinds of plants and animals than the Coast Redwoods. Only two species—the chickaree, a type of squirrel, and the long-horned wood-boring beetle, a small insect— feed on any part of the big trees. In doing so, they help the trees reproduce.

The chickaree eats the scales of the Giant Sequoia cones. While feeding, it drops many seeds on the ground, where a few sprout into new saplings. The squirrel also buries some cones to eat later. Some of these are forgotten, and they, too, grow into new trees.

The beetle—which is only about as long as a ladybug—also helps new Giant Sequoia to grow. The beetle lays its eggs on the cones. When the eggs hatch, the larvae bore into the cone and eat it. This kills part of the cone and releases the seeds, which fall to the ground to become new trees.

Dozens of other species live in the Giant Sequoia groves. Larger animals there include the mule deer, mountain lion, wolverine, pine marten, coyote, bobcat and fisher. Among the smaller animals found there are the deer mouse and gray squirrel. At least 30 kinds of birds breed in the Giant Sequoia groves, and many more visit them.

The Giant Sequoias share their high mountain valleys with other trees, such as the ponderosa pine, western yew, sugar pine, Douglas fir and incense cedar. Ferns carpet the forest floor, and wildflowers such as buttercups, lupine, wild strawberries, trillium and mariposa lilies add spots of color between the rusty-red trunks.

Some species—such as the mountain lion, coyote, Douglas fir and sword fern—also exist in the Coast Redwood forests. But the taller redwood also hosts many other species.

The playful river otter likes the many rivers and streams of the North Coast, and the raccoon also lives there. But the most majestic species found among the Coast Redwoods—and not in the Giant Sequoias—is the Roosevelt elk, named after President Theodore Roosevelt. Once very rare, the elk has built up its

numbers in a few parts of the northern range of the Coast Redwood. But it still is absent from the southern range around San Francisco and from the Santa Cruz and Big Sur areas even farther south.

The southern redwoods are home to the wild boar, which was brought to California from Europe. Blacktail deer romp throughout all of the range of the Coast Redwood.

Many kinds of plants grow among the Coast Redwoods. They include trees such as the tan oak, big-leaf maple and western hemlock, and shrubs such as the azalea, rhododendron and California huckleberry. Ferns cover the forest floor along with redwood sorrel, bunchberry dogwood and other species.

Both kinds of redwood forests are "climax communities"—or at least they were until logging began. That means no new species will naturally come along and replace them. The Tree Giants live in harmony with the plants and animals that have adapted to their domain.

The Mythical Forest

Because of the redwood's remarkable size, and because of the unearthly stillness that fills a dense redwood forest, the Tree Giants have been the source of many myths and legends. The redwood forest is full of magic and mythical creatures.

Native Indian tribes worshipped the great trees. Some drank the sap hoping to gain magical powers. Others thought the giants were actually great warriors who had turned to redwood. And others thought their medicine men haunted the redwood forests at night in the form of a grizzly bear.

Gnomes have been said to dwell among the redwoods, making their tiny homes at the base of the tall trees. These little people live for several hundred years and grow to be only 5 or 6 inches tall. They are friendly with all the creatures of the forest, it is said.

Mariposa was a beautiful fairy princess who traveled far and wide until she met a fairy prince who lived in the redwood forest. She fell in love with him and spent the rest of her days among the Tree Giants, painting little spots on the white flower which today is known as the mariposa lily.

Even leprechauns are said to have found their way to the redwood forests after all the trees in Ireland were cut down.

One legendary figure as huge as the trees themselves is Paul Bunyan. He moved west from Minnesota with his blue ox, Babe, clearing state after state of its trees so that settlers could build their homes—so the legend says. Of course, Paul visited Redwood Country.

The Ewok is a more recent dweller in the heart of the redwood forest. Lucasfilm Ltd. created this teddy-bear-like creature in the 1980s, for the movie *The Return of the Jedi*. The Ewoks ruled the forest moon, Endor, which looked much like a forest of Coast Redwoods, where the film was shot.

Who knows how many more elves, spirits and other mysterious little creatures live among the giant redwoods?

Using the Redwoods

Native Indian tribes had many uses for redwood. They built shelters from its bark and from planks they made by splitting the giant trunks. They made redwood canoes, and they shredded the bark to make skirts and baskets.

Still, the Indians barely made a dent in the vast stands of Coast Redwood and Giant Sequoia. In fact, they rarely cut down redwoods, preferring instead to use fallen trees.

When white settlers moved to California, they quickly discovered that redwood made an excellent building material. It resists insects, fungi, fire, and decay. It has an unusually straight grain that makes it strong and attractive.

These rare qualities make redwood popular for building things that get wet often, such as decks, patios, hot tubs, planters, fences and siding. Many buildings constructed by California settlers a century ago still stand today as proof of the durability of redwood.

Virgin or "old-growth" Coast Redwoods are stronger and more prized as lumber than "second-growth" redwoods which have sprung up after the virgin forests were cut. Today, most redwood sold in lumberyards comes from second-growth trees. It is still beautiful and durable, but not quite as strong as old-growth redwood lumber.

A Challenge for Loggers

The early Indians, who had no metal tools, developed an amazing way to cut down redwoods. They used heated rocks to burn a ring around the massive trunk, and then they scraped away the charred wood. They repeated this process over and over until the giant tumbled to the earth. Each tree probably took weeks to fell.

Indian logging practices had little impact on the redwood groves. But then white settlers realized the economic value of redwood trees. At first, timber companies thought the redwood was too soft and light to use for building. Then they discovered its strength, beauty and incredible durability, and they began cutting trees as fast as possible.

At first, loggers used oxen and horses to haul the massive trees out of the woods. In 1881, a steam-driven contraption called the Dolbeer Donkey replaced the oxen and horses. Still, getting the heavy logs out of the woods and to sawmills was very difficult. Then, in the early 1930s, the first "cat" came to Redwood Country. With this gasoline-powered tractor, it was easier to remove the trees.

In the early years, ships hauled redwood lumber to ports all over the world. In 1914, the railroad came to haul logs out of Redwood Country. Then, in the 1930s, the logging truck arrived, and the pace of tree removal increased even more.

Until the 1930s, loggers used axes and crosscut saws to cut down the big trees. It took three to five days to cut down one tree. When the gasoline-driven chain saw found its way to the redwood groves, loggers could fell a tree in just two hours.

The Coast Redwood was much easier to cut down than the Giant Sequoia because it was not as fat. It also was more "shatterproof," and did not break into small pieces when it crashed to the earth. The Coast Redwood also grew in thick forests near rivers and the coastline which made removal much easier.

Protecting the Survivors

The redwoods have always had protectors. Long ago, they were the native Indians who worshipped the big trees. Today, modern environmentalists have taken up the cause.

The redwoods did not really need protection until the late 1800s, when loggers began cutting down the Tree Giants so rapidly that some people feared the redwood forests might completely disappear.

The Giant Sequoias were much easier to protect than the Coast Redwoods. The Giant Sequoias grew among the spectacular scenery of the Sierra Nevada. And these trees were not as useful for building. So logging companies did not put up much of a fight when environmentalists wanted to protect the big trees.

Congress created Sequoia, General Grant and Yosemite national parks in 1890. In 1940, it included General Grant in a new park called Kings Canyon. Sequoia and Sierra national forests also protected their groves of old-growth redwoods until, eventually, 92 percent of the biggest and best Giant Sequoias were safely enclosed in federal and state parks and national forests.

But, environmentalists had to work much harder to preserve some of the last of the Coast Redwoods. The State of California started protecting them in 1901 by setting aside a group of outstanding trees in the Santa Cruz Mountains in an area now called Big Basin State Park. Today, California has 32 state redwood parks, thanks in large part to the Save-the-Redwoods League. Siskouyou, Six Rivers, and Los Padres national forests also protect small groves of Coast Redwoods.

In 1906, the federal government created the Monterey Forest Reserve in the Santa Cruz Mountains. In 1908, a local business-man, William Kent, donated 503 acres of redwoods just north of San Francisco to the federal government. This grove, known as Muir Woods National Monument, has more visitors than any other redwood park.

An even more intense conflict erupted over the creation of Redwood National Park in northern California. Many people who lived there did not want a national park because their jobs depended on continued logging of old-growth Coast Redwoods.

The Save-the-Redwoods League and the Sierra Club (which was founded by John Muir), along with many other conservation groups, fought to establish the park. In 1968, they won. Although the new Redwood National Park was only half as big as they had wanted (58,000 acres), it contained the world's tallest trees.

But, the fight was not over. Logging companies continued to cut redwoods along the boundaries of the park. Their operations disrupted the land, caused erosion and threatened the park redwoods. Ten years later, conservationists finally convinced Congress to enlarge the park to 106,000 acres.

Even now, the drive to protect the redwoods goes on. In the beginning, California had 2 million acres of Coast Redwoods. Eighty-five percent of the virgin forests have been cut. Another 10 percent have been protected in national and state parks and national forests, but that means 5 percent still are unprotected.

The Save-the-Redwoods League continues to raise money to buy some of these unprotected redwoods. If the League succeeds, more Tree Giants—the old-growth redwood trees—will survive. If they don't succeed, more will perish.

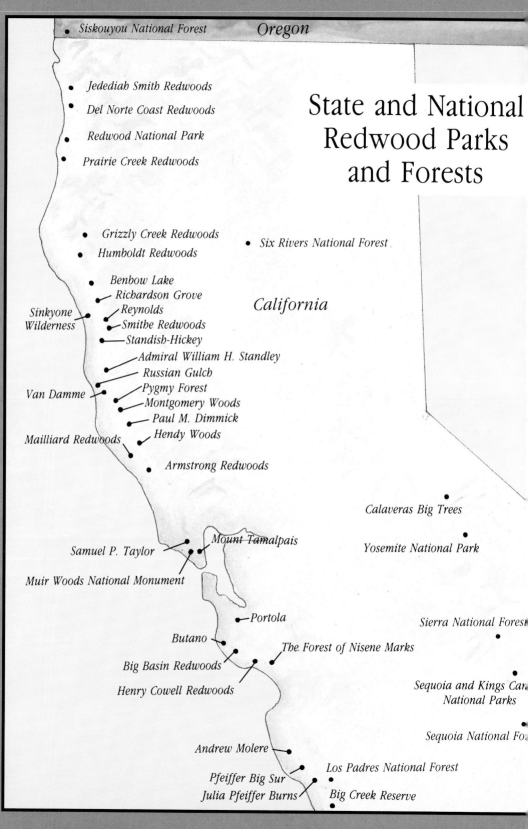

Siskouyou National Forest — Oregon

State and National
Redwood Parks
and Forests

Jedediah Smith Redwoods
Del Norte Coast Redwoods
Redwood National Park
Prairie Creek Redwoods

Grizzly Creek Redwoods
Humboldt Redwoods
Six Rivers National Forest

Benbow Lake
Richardson Grove
Reynolds
Sinkyone Wilderness
Smithe Redwoods
Standish-Hickey

California

Admiral William H. Standley
Russian Gulch
Van Damme
Pygmy Forest
Montgomery Woods
Paul M. Dimmick
Hendy Woods
Mailliard Redwoods
Armstrong Redwoods

Calaveras Big Trees

Yosemite National Park

Mount Tamalpais
Samuel P. Taylor
Muir Woods National Monument

Portola
Sierra National Forest
Butano
The Forest of Nisene Marks
Big Basin Redwoods
Henry Cowell Redwoods
Sequoia and Kings Canyon
National Parks

Sequoia National Forest

Andrew Molere
Los Padres National Forest
Pfeiffer Big Sur
Julia Pfeiffer Burns
Big Creek Reserve

Where to See Redwoods

Fortunately, many outstanding redwood groves are protected in state and federal parks and national forests. These areas have campgrounds, picnic areas, nature trails and other services to help visitors see and understand the giant trees.

For More Information

Several national and state nonprofit organizations have been working for years to protect redwoods and provide information on these remarkable trees. You can get this information by contacting the following organizations:

Redwood Natural History Association
Redwood National Park
1111 Second Street
Crescent City, CA 95531
Phone: 707-464-9150

Sequoia Natural History Association
Sequoia National Park
Ash Mountain, P.O. Box 10
Three Rivers, CA 93271
Phone: 209-565-3344

The Yosemite Association
P.O. Box 545
Yosemite National Park, CA 95389
Phone: 209-379-2646

**National Forest
Interpretive Association**
USDA-Forest Service
630 Sansome Street
San Francisco, CA 94111
Phone: 415-556-1658

Calaveras Big Tree Association
Calaveras Big Tree State Park
P.O. Box 120
Arnold, CA 95223
Phone; 209-795-2334

Humboldt Redwoods Interpretive Association
Humboldt Redwoods State Park
P.O. Box 100
Weott, CA 95571
Phone: 707-946-2311

**North Coast Redwoods
Interpretive Association**
Prairie Creek Redwoods State Park
3431 Fort Avenue
Eureka, CA 95501
Phone: 707-488-2171

**Northern Counties Logging
Interpretive Association**
Fort Humboldt State Historic Park
3431 Fort Avenue
Eureka, CA 95501
Phone: 707-445-6567

**Santa Cruz Mountains
Natural History Association**
Santa Cruz Mountains Area
101 N. Big Trees Road
Felton, CA 95018
Phone: 408-335-3174

Save-the-Redwoods League
Suite 605, 114 Sansome Street
San Francisco, CA 94104
Phone: 415-362-2352

Northwest Interpretive Association
Siskouyou National Forest
Six Rivers National Forest
83 S. King Street, Rm. 212
Seattle, WA 98107
Phone: 206-442-7958

Los Padres Interpretive Association
Los Padres National Forest
P.O. Box 3502
Santa Barbara, CA 93105
Phone: 805-962-9730

Three Forest Interpretive Association
Sequoia National Forest
Sierra National Forest
13098 E. Wiregrass Lane
Clovis, CA 93612
Phone: 209-229-4017